Christmas 2002

Vickie—

How blessed I am to have you
as my friend. Thank you for being
the best girlfriend in the world.

I love you.

Heather

tIM McGraW

and the dancehall doctors

+im mcGraw

and the dancehall doctors

This is Ours.

Tim McGraw

with Martin Huxley

ATRIA BOOKS

New York   London   Toronto   Sydney   Singapore

ATRIA BOOKS
1230 Avenue of the Americas
New York, NY 10020

Art Direction and Design: Glenn Sweitzer for fresh design
Creative Direction: Kelly Clague Wright

Cover photography: Marina Chavez, Miami, FL 2002
Cover illustration: Glenn Sweitzer for fresh design
Map with signatures on endpapers and page 89 courtesy of Joey Supak

Copyright © 2002 by Tim McGraw

Catskills map reproduced with permission of JIMAPCO, Inc.
Copyright © 2000

All rights reserved, including the right to reproduce
this book or portions thereof in any form whatsoever.
For information address Atria Books, 1230 Avenue
of the Americas, New York, NY 10020

ISBN: 0-7434-6706-X

First Atria Books hardcover printing November 2002

10 9 8 7 6 5 4 3 2 1

ATRIA BOOKS is a trademark of Simon & Schuster, Inc.

For information regarding special discounts for bulk purchases,
please contact Simon & Schuster Special Sales at 1-800-456-6798 or
business@simonandschuster.com

Printed in the U.S.A.

Further photo credits can be found on page 164.

*When we first started this
project, I felt like I was doing
something good for the band.
But actually it turned out
that they did something good
for me, for themselves
and for our careers. I feel like
this is the greatest music
we've ever made together.*

— Tim

contents

the vision

Over the past ten years, I've been fortunate enough to have more success as a performer and recording artist than I'd ever dreamed. I've always tried to continue growing and evolving as an artist, and to keep coming up with new challenges to keep myself focused and moving forward. I'm proud of every record I've ever made, but there are certain things that I've always wanted to do with my records that I'd never completely achieved.

There's a specific way that records generally get made. Usually, the singer is backed in the studio by studio musicians, rather than by the band musicians who accompany the singer on the road. In other words, the guys that the fans see playing on stage are almost never the same ones who play on the original record.

Session players are some of the best musicians anywhere; they can just walk in and nail their parts right off the bat and we've made some cool records that way. It's different than the organic vibe that you get from a real band playing together—a bunch of guys who have a unique history in common, who have lived together in the back of a van and played music together in every kind of place imaginable—from dumpy night clubs to stadiums.

My first six albums were done in pretty much the standard way—the session guys came in and laid down the tracks and I sang over them. And as much as I love and am proud of all of those records, there was always a little something missing for me. The records that I loved when I was growing up had more than great songs; they had a feel, a groove, a vibe. It's not something you can put your finger on; you hear old Rolling Stones records and they're *great,* but you can't just pick an individual part and point to *why* it's great. It's the whole deal, and when you listen with your heart, you just catch that wave. I've always wanted to capture that kind of feeling on my own records.

That's why I decided to record my seventh studio album with my live band, the Dancehall Doctors. My guys have been with me for a long time and they're an important element of what I do, so it was time to try and capture that on a record. This is something I've been wanting to do for years, and it just felt like this was the right time to do it.

I wanted it to be a team effort, and I wanted to capture something that had heart and soul all the way through. I think we've done that on this record. We wanted to really capture the excitement of that '70s groove that you hear on Allman Brothers records or Eagles records. Not that we were trying to be retro or sound like those guys; we just wanted to combine that kind of atmosphere and energy with a modern sound. The synergy that we have on stage has always been an important thing for me. Before I started having success with my records, the live thing was the biggest catalyst in my career. The thing that kept me going was what we did live and the response we got, and I always tried to keep that sound in my head when I made records. I wanted to make a record where it's not just about me, where there's soul all the way through. And to get that, I needed my band.

In some ways, this record is the culmination of the thing that we've been working at for the last ten years, becoming a band and working together as a team. It's also the most fun I've ever had making a record. After seven albums, you just want to try something different. I wanted to make music that's more organic, and it felt like the best way to make that happen was to record with my guys. For the step that I wanted to take in our music, this was obviously the way to go.

I'm always looking for ways to have fun and keep it fresh and create new challenges for myself, just because I don't want to make the same record every year. I get bored very easily, and if I start getting bored with the stuff that I'm doing, then I figure other people will get bored, too. If you get complacent and start liking what you do too much, it's not going to get any better or make any progress. I could have gone in and cut just another record, but I'd rather do something that makes somebody go, "Hey, that's cool, I want to hear this."

I've always felt like everybody expected us to fail on every record. I think that now we've finally gotten past that to a point where everybody kind of expects our records to be good. So it seemed like a good time to say, "Okay, let's take the band up to a studio in the mountains and see what we come up with, and let's see what they think of *that*." When people are expecting it to be good, then you need to come up with new ways to knock people out.

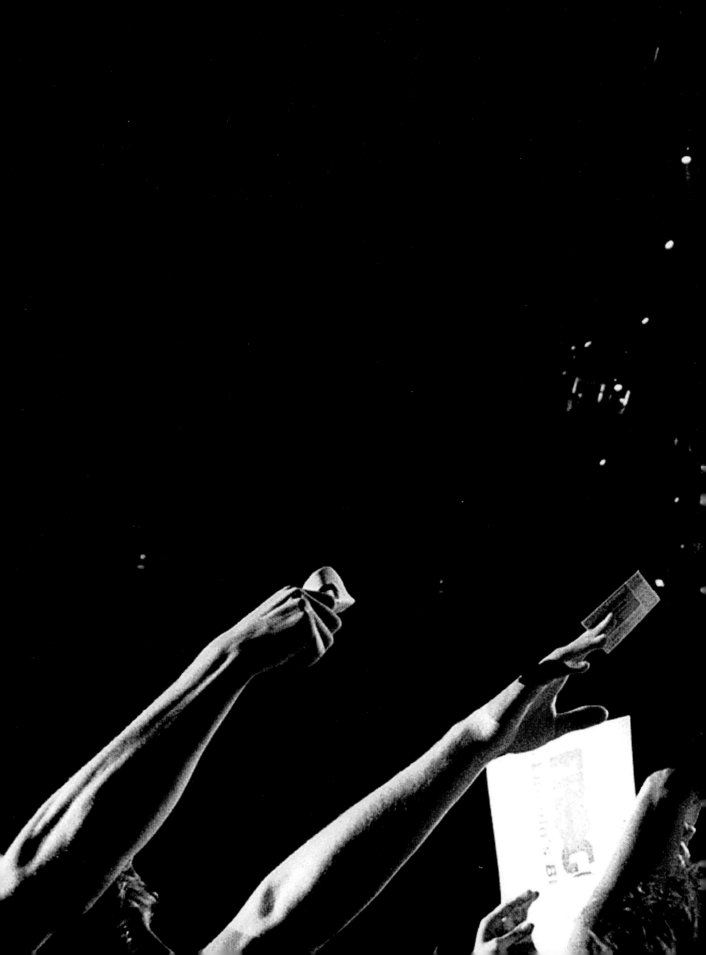

When I first told everybody what I wanted to do on this record, I did encounter some resistance. People can be afraid to take chances when there's money being spent on things like studio time. But the people who worried about that are the same people who worry about every record that I make, so it didn't concern me too much.

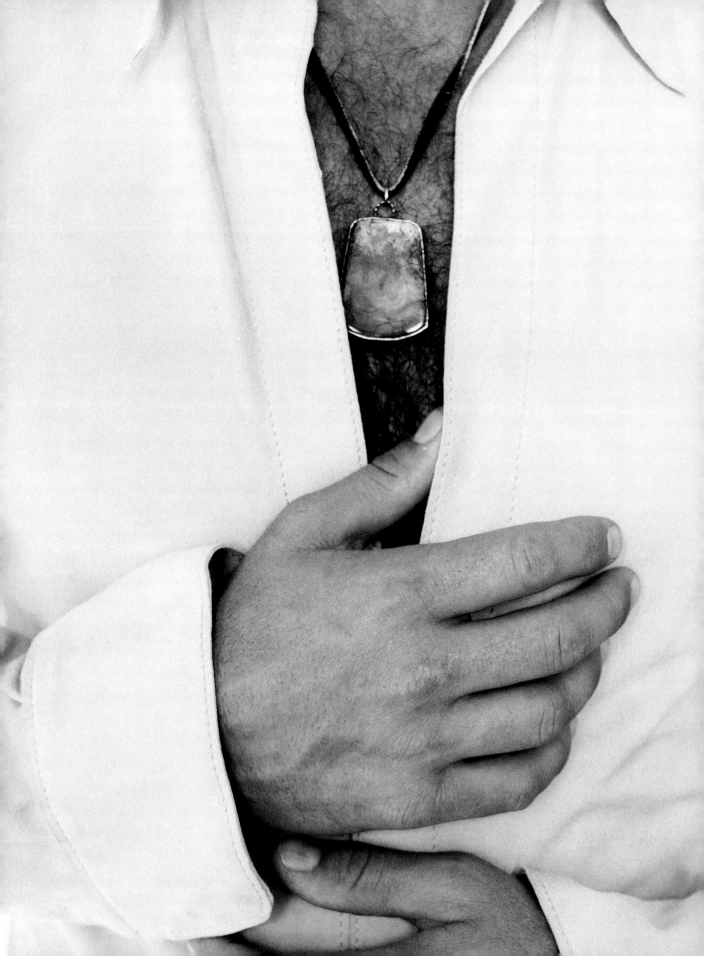

Darran Smith, lead guitarist and band leader: I think the natural inclination in Nashville is that they don't like to mess with success—if it ain't broke, don't fix it. So everybody's records end up sounding the same, because it's the same group of A-list guys playing on every record.

Jeff McMahon, keyboards: I think that Nashville kind of lends itself to a group mentality, to the point that even the biggest artists are afraid to color outside the lines and blaze a new trail. But Tim's not afraid of that; if anything, he gets off on stepping out there and taking a chance, because he's got confidence in his vision. It's hard to fight the Nashville music machine, and I think it takes somebody with the clout that Tim has to put his neck on the line and say, "Look, I'm going to try something different." I think it made some jaws drop when Tim said he was going to use his road band on the record, because that's just not the way things are done in Nashville. Everybody's excited about the record now, but at the beginning there was no reason for them to want to support it, because they were looking at all the years of success he's had, which had nothing to do with us playing on the records. Tim was pretty much on his own, leading the charge of us wanting to do it.

Mark Hurt, co-manager: It's been Tim's mission for years to make a record with his band, and that is completely out of the norm for a country artist. In Nashville, there's a big gap between the guys that play on records and the guys that get on a bus and do the shows; it's like the difference between playing in the world series and playing double-A ball. I don't personally agree with it, but it's become so embedded into my thought processes because it's the way things have been done for so long and it's just so omnipresent.

Scott Siman, co-manager: Yeah, I've seen a lot of raised eyebrows, and I think that people in Nashville are going "Why's he upsetting the apple cart?" So often in music, you hear people say they want to be different, but then they never really go do anything about it. They usually end up going with the safe choice and doing the three-and-a-half-minute up-tempo country love song and putting the big headshot on the album cover. There's so many things that you can default to when the heat is on. And here's an artist who's at the top of his game, who doesn't have to take

any risks, saying, "No, I want to push the envelope." In country music, that's unprecedented. He didn't need to bring this kind of grief and stress into his life to go spend three months

that and he followed through with it. Tim understood the risks, and he understood the effort that it would take, but he said, "This is what I need to do." I think that Tim's the musi-

picks the best material, and he's the one that takes chances. So a lot of people are looking to him and going, "Hey, what's Tim doing? What's his new thing?" It would have been easy for Tim to just to go back in the studio and do the same old same old, but instead he decided to take a huge leap creatively and do something that's outside the box. And so that was the framework from which we operated with this record, trying to make his vision a reality and seeing where it leads us.

So yeah, there may have been some resistance, but I didn't want to know about it because I was going to do this anyway. One person who didn't resist was my longtime friend and co-producer, Byron Gallimore. Byron was confident in the project from the very start. Here's a guy who could have the biggest ego of all—with all the success he's had. But that's just not Byron. He and I have worked together a long time and he really knows me and he knows the band. He has been out to hundreds of shows through the years and he's paid attention to the guys. Part of what makes Byron a great producer is that he's an incredible musician—so you know he's been paying attention to what the band has been playing and to what they've been bringing to the table in live shows. If he didn't believe that

they could do it, he would have said something. But he was right with me on the project from the start. He understood the risks as well as, if not better than, anyone. But he was confident.

Sure, everybody felt like it was risky. Even I felt like it was risky; still probably did until we heard the final mixes. In the end, I think the feeling that it was risky created a positive energy that solidified the feeling that we were going to go in there and make a great record. A lot of people don't think it's possible to make a record that's cool and commercial, but I think we've proven that it can be done. Once the ball started rolling, everybody seemed to figure out what we were trying to do and then got excited about it. And now that it's done, I think that everybody is turning backflips and breathing deep sighs of relief. The thing is, I love doing this so much, and I look at it as a challenge to keep getting better. I hear things and I think, "Wow, it would be cool to try that," or I listen to my last record and think that now I've got a better idea of how to get where I was trying to go. To me, this is my life's work—besides my marriage and my kids—so I have to take it seriously, and I want to keep building on it.

this album is **Ours**

the dancehall doctors

"Our first drummer, Randy Davis, came up with the name the Dancehall Doctors. It's from a Conway Twitty song. It came up when we were doing that first gig in Delaware, long before Tim ever had a deal or anything, and we've been called that ever since."

—Darran Smith

the dancehall doctors tm dhd

Most of the guys in the Dancehall Doctors have been playing with me for between ten and fifteen years— the newest member joined eight years ago. There aren't a lot of bands out there who've been together that long, and I'm really proud of that. I've got a lot of history with these guys, and that helps to keep me in touch with the reasons that I first started doing this. It's hard to pull a star trip on guys who knew you when you were borrowing money from them. I still love hanging out with them as much as I love playing with them.

For the first couple of years, we had a whole different band; Bob was there, and Jeff was there for part of that. Right before *Not a Moment Too Soon* came out, just before "Indian Outlaw" hit, the rest of the band quit. We were going, "This is not a good time to quit, I swear something's about to happen." And they were like, "Oh, we're burned, nothing's gonna happen."

When I was starting out, I didn't really have a specific concept of the kind of band I wanted, I just knew the kind of people that I liked. I wanted guys who'd want to go out and play, and who'd understand my way of thinking about how to make music. At first, it was just whoever I could find who'd take the job. But by the time we got the right people and finally locked it all together, we had some serious mutual respect between all of us, about the jobs that we do and what it takes to get those jobs done.

One thing that I knew from the start was that I didn't want to have the kind of band where it's the one guy out front with a bunch of anony-mous guys wearing black back in the shadows. To me, that's not a band. I've always felt that if you're going to surround yourself with people who are creative, why wouldn't you want their input? I want people around me who are going to bring something to the party in terms of talent, person-ality, and musical ideas. I might argue with them about things, but that doesn't mean I don't want to hear their opinions.

Everybody in this band is a great player individually, everybody's back-ground is a little different, and every-body's got his own little niche. But there's also this serious common ground that we share, and that comes out in the music that we make together. They're all guys from different parts of the country who came to Nashville because they loved music, and their love of music is still the thing that motivates them. And that motivates me. They drive me to be the best that I can be.

Darran Smith

I grew up in Kansas, got an old Sears guitar when I was eight, and started playing in bands in my early teens— country, '50s rock 'n' roll, southern rock, a little of everything. Eventually a drummer friend talked me into coming down to Nashville for awhile to check things out. I came down here in 1982, did a couple of little session things and moved to Nashville permanently in '83. It was pretty tight for awhile, working day jobs, doing construction and whatever I had to do to get by. I ended up landing a house gig at this hotel lounge and played there for three and a half years. I met Tim in '89; he'd just moved to Nashville and didn't have much going on. I was playing another house gig over at a place called Sissy's and also was playing down in Printers Alley at this club called Skull's Rainbow Room. Tim used to hang down there all the time, and he asked me if I wanted to go play for three or four days in a club up in Delaware.

FAVORITE TIM CUT:
"Please Remember Me"

FAVORITE SONG ON THE NEW ALBUM:
"She's My Kind of Rain"

FAVORITE SONG EVER:
Sammy Hagar & Van Halen's "Finish What You Started"

John Marcus

{ b a s s }

I grew up in Florida in a musical family. I started playing clarinet in fourth grade, and I hated it because the Beatles and Monkees had just come out and I wanted to play guitar. So I got an acoustic guitar, picked up a Mel Bay book, and started banging out chords. When I was in the sixth or seventh grade, I hooked up with some kids down the street who had a little garage band; they already had a guitar player, a drummer, and a keyboard player, so I picked up a bass for, like, fifty bucks and it was love instantly. I got really serious about bass, listening to guys like Stanley Clarke and Jaco Pastorius and playing rock 'n' roll and jazz. My older brothers were into some pretty weird stuff and knew a lot of serious jazz guys, and they were a pretty big influence on me. In the middle '70s, I joined a rock band called Fantasy that had been signed and had had a hit record and were trying to regain their former glory, and it just came to the point where I hated rock 'n' roll and didn't want to play it anymore. I'd always sworn that I would never play country music, but I met these bluegrass guys who played like nothing I had ever heard in my life and I said, "OK, this is cool." I also played in Tanya Tucker's band for awhile. Then a friend of mine said he knew this guy named Tim who needed a bass player, so I went and did a couple of things with him. He said, "We're not gonna rehearse, let's just go out and wing it." And I said, "This is for me."

FAVORITE TIM CUT:
"For a Little While"

FAVORITE SONG ON THE NEW ALBUM:
"Sleep Tonight"

FAVORITE SONG EVER:
Graham Central Station's "Release Yourself"

Bob Minner

{ a c o u s t i c g u i t a r,
d o b r o, b a n j o }

I grew up in Missouri and started playing banjo when I was five; my first professional gig was playing at the opening of a carpet store when I was ten, and I played bluegrass banjo and electric guitar through high school. In the late '80s I was doing forty weeks a year playing Holiday Inns and country saloons with a band that included a drummer named Randy Davis, whose dad, Gene Davis, is a really big West Coast country music pioneer. Around 1990, Randy left the band to move to Nashville; a few months later my wife and I visited Nashville for a few days and stayed with Randy and his roommate, who was Tim. Tim was just pluggin' around town; he didn't even have a demo yet, but he definitely had the charisma. My wife said, "If that guy ever does anything, he'll be a star." He definitely had the charisma back then. We came off the road when my wife had our first son, and Tim was calling me asking me to do these club dates with him and Randy, but I'd already committed to a day job retreading tires, so I stuck with that. That's when Tim found Darran and hired him. I didn't enjoy retreading tires much, and one day I flipped on CMT and saw Tim's first video, "Welcome to the Club." So I called him and told him that I also played acoustic, and he hired me.

FAVORITE TIM CUT:
"Set This Circus Down"

FAVORITE ON THE NEW ALBUM:
"Watch the Wind Blow By"

FAVORITE SONG EVER:
"Enough" written by my wife, Ginger.
She is a great Christian writer, and that song always
brings me back to square one concerning humbleness.

Jeff
McMahon

{keyboards, background vocals}

I grew up in Gainesville, Texas, playing piano and stuff in school. It was a small town and I didn't know guitar players and people like that; the people that I knew were all in band or choir in school. I went to Baylor University and I wound up playing in my first country band with a couple of college buddies, Brett Beavers and Deryl Dodd, who later moved to Nashville and had their songs cut by Tim. When that band broke up I moved to Nashville and worked with a guy named Butch Baker, then with a group called Canyon for about a year and then started doing some showcase work for some writers that worked for Byron Gallimore's publishing company, which is how I met Tim. Byron was one of the people that recommended me to Tim. I auditioned for Tim and started playing with him in March of '93. When he hired me I think it was as much for the fact that I'm real physical on stage as it was for my playing. The day Tim hired me, he was at Deryl Dodd's birthday party and ran into a guy that I had worked for before, and this guy told Tim, "Man, I don't know if you want to hire that McMahon guy because he's really flashy onstage and he'll just try to steal the spotlight." And Tim told me he thought that that was a great reason to hire me.

FAVORITE TIM CUT:
"Carry On"

FAVORITE SONG ON THE NEW ALBUM:
"That's Why God Made Mexico"

FAVORITE SONG OF ALL TIME:
Jackson Browne's "The Load Out"

Dean Brown

{fiddle, mandolin, acoustic guitar, cello, background vocals}

I grew up in Texas in the Rio Grande Valley, about twenty-five minutes north of the Mexican border. I started playing classical violin when I was eight years old, and started playing country in my early teens. I moved to Nashville in 1992 and kicked around for a while, playing talent contests and working in retail to keep myself going. I actually met Tim through a mutual friend before I moved to Nashville, while I was visiting. He'd been in town for a week or two, playing around town doing open mikes, and we just hit it off. Back then, Tim was new in Nashville and nothing was really happening for him. But he had this confidence that made you feel like he knew it was going to work out, that everything was going to be cool. We'd sit in his little apartment for hours playing video games or watching movies. He'd call me up and say, "Hey, what are you doin'?" "Nothing." "Well, come on over, and bring a fire log." His deal was always to bring a fire log, because sometimes there was no heat. It seemed like he didn't worry about day-to-day things like paying the electric bill, because he just felt like things were going to work out. But he'd give anybody his last five dollars if he knew they needed it or if anybody came to ask him. He was a very shy, humble kind of a guy, but when he'd get on stage, he just came alive; it was like a different person.

FAVORITE TIM CUT:
"Just To See you Smile"

FAVORITE SONG ON THE NEW ALBUM:
"Comfort Me"

FAVORITE SONG OF ALL TIME:
James Taylor's "Fire and Rain"

Denny
Hemingson

{steel guitar,
acoustic & electric guitar}

I grew up in Sioux City, Iowa, and when I got out of school I moved up to Minneapolis and played in local bands up there for a few years. Then I moved to Honolulu because it's way too cold in Minneapolis, and I played in clubs for tourists and stuff, playing whatever I had to play to get a gig. Eventually, I realized that I needed to get to a major music city to progress, so I moved to Nashville and did some clubs and sessions and stuff. The first touring gig I got was with Paulette Carlson, who had been the lead singer for Highway 101; Billy Mason was in that band, too. I did that for awhile, until the opportunity to join Tim's band arose, and I've been here ever since.

FAVORITE TIM CUT:
"Cowboy In Me"

FAVORITE SONG ON NEW ALBUM:
"She's My Kind of Rain"

FAVORITE SONG OF ALL TIME:
John Coltrane's "Naima"

Billy Mason

{ **d r u m s** }

I was born in Cleveland and grew up in Los Angeles. Before Tim, I'd played with a pretty diverse bunch of artists, including Jo-El Sonnier, Clarence "Gatemouth" Brown, and Paulette Carlson, which is where I met Denny. Paulette took some time off and I was doing this club date with another artist and Darran was in the band, and he told me he was working with this new guy, Tim McGraw, and that they needed a drummer. We all met at Byron's studio and Tim heard me play and hired me. I figured I'd do the gig for a few months, and I've been here for eight and a half years now.

FAVORITE TIM CUT:
"Somebody's Prayin"

FAVORITE SONG ON THE NEW ALBUM:
"Illegal"

FAVORITE SONG OF ALL TIME:
Barry Manilow's "Ready to Take a Chance Again"

David Dunkley

{percussion, background vocals}

I started out doing the bar scene in my hometown of Charleston, West Virginia, and writing and trying to send stuff to Nashville. I packed up and moved to Nashville in '87, went back home to lick my wounds in '88, came back again in '92, and went back home again a year later. I was back in Charleston in '95 and playing drums in a rock band and I got a call from our sound man, John Ward, who's also West Virginia. He knew I knew how to tune a drum set and make it sound good, so he called to see if I wanted to come be a drum tech with Tim for a couple of weeks, and after that I never went back home. After I'd been on the crew for about a year, I started playing percussion on a few songs during the show, which meant that I'd be tech-ing for Billy through the show, then change my shirt, push the congas out from under the drum riser and play them on the song, then push them back underneath, change my clothes, and take the drums and pack them up. Then Tim started talking about adding a full-time percussionist, and Darran says, "You've already got someone capable working for you." So one day Tim just walked by me in the hallway and said, "I want you to order up everything you need so you can start playing in the band full time." My first full-time gig with the band was at the Universal Ampitheatre in LA, which was a little intimidating.

FAVORITE TIM CUT:
"Wrong Man"

FAVORITE SONG ON THE NEW ALBUM:
"All We Ever Find"

FAVORITE SONG EVER:
The Isley Brothers's "Voyage to Atlantis"

The **D**ance hall Doct**O**rs

Darran Smith: Back then, Tim was pretty much the same guy he is now, but he was still finding himself as a singer, and still kind of emulating Clint Black, George Strait, and Garth Brooks. His career wasn't really happening yet, and everybody was telling me, "Why do you wanna hang with that guy? He ain't makin' no money," and I'd say, "I don't know, there's just something about him." Even back then he had that cocky, confident thing—not arrogant, but you knew he knew what he wanted as far as career goes. He was still trying to figure out how to do it, but he had that air of confidence. Things were pretty tight for a while; for a long time, it was just me and Tim in a van and trailer. Johnboy was there for a while in the early days, but he quit to play with the Remingtons, because he thought they were going to be a huge success. He eventually came to his senses and we let him come back.

3

the journey

"I'm a country singer because of the way I sing, but I was influenced by a lot of different music, so there's a lot of rock 'n' roll in there too."

tim mcgraw
a place in the sun

TIM McGRAW

TIM McGRAW
set this circus down

I realize that I'm part of the mainstream country music business, because I've had some success. But I don't *feel* like I'm part of the mainstream country music business. I mean, I love Nashville, and there's some great people there who know a lot about making great records, but I'm not interested in chasing after the same thing as everybody else or feeling like I have to be part of the "in" crowd. And that's fine, because I like *my* crowd. My friends in Nashville are the guys in the band, my producer, my crew guys and a few other artists. As far as knowing the system of Nashville and knowing who's what and who's powerful, I don't. I couldn't tell you the names of the label heads, I can't tell you the names of the hot songwriters in Nashville, I don't know who the big producers are. That's just not on my radar.

I do think of myself as a serious artist, but I don't think it's productive to dwell on that too much. I've always just tried to be myself and do what feels right for me. I think that the best thing I can do as an artist is to make sure I'm having a good time and hope that that shows through. I listen to the radio and buy CDs. I consider myself a music fan. I know what I like to hear on the radio, so that probably guides me. I just assume that if it pleases me, other people will pick up on that. Whether you're a painter or a carpenter or whatever kind of

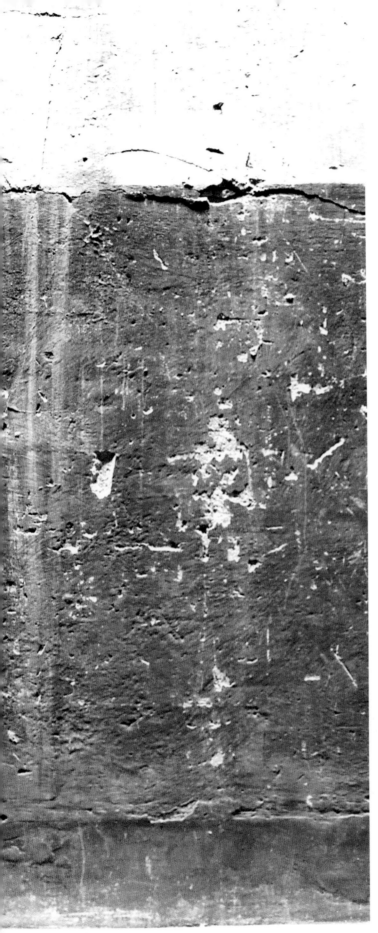

artist you are, I think that if you love what you do, it shows up in your work.

If you look back at some of the biggest and most influential artists, the guys who changed musical history, they're usually the guys that nobody understood at the time. Hank Williams was one of the most important country guys ever and probably the first rock star. He wasn't a conventional singer—he did things his way and sang songs the way he felt them—and the country music establishment at the time *hated* him. The same with Elvis; people were telling him what to do and how to do it, but he understood what he needed to be doing. I'm not comparing myself to those guys—they're my idols, they're legends. They're the reminder that we all have to just do what we do and not concentrate so much on what everyone around us is thinking or saying.

I feel like I'm trying to make a kind of American music—the kind of music that guys in the bar feel like they can listen to and relate to, and that their wives and girlfriends can also relate to, without feeling like I'm some movie star kind of guy that's out of the realm of their reality. It's just the music we play. I'm a country singer because of the way I sing, but I was influenced by a lot of different music, so there's a lot of rock 'n' roll in there, too. It's the same with the way these guys

play. They've all played lots of different kinds of music, and all of those influences show up in what we do together.

Mark Hurt: Tim's one of the few artists in the country music genre who rises above the comic-book-character thing. He's a legitimate artist. I think he's a little uncomfortable talking about himself in those terms, but he's very serious and introspective about what he does, and he has a very clear perspective on what works for him. When a guy and a girl come to a Tim McGraw concert, the guy wants to go backstage and have some beers with him and the girl wants to take him home to mom. That's a hell of a balance to find, but he seems to have a

natural ability for that.

Scott Siman: Tim always says, "I don't make music for critics, I'm just trying to make the record that I hear in my head." I think every artist wants to have critical acclaim and commercial success. But when all is said and done, I think Tim really would rather have an album that he's proud of, and an album that they can look back on fifteen years from now and go, "I'm proud of that record, I still want to sing those songs." I think that Tim's keenly aware of the kind of legacy he wants to leave behind. I think he's striving really hard to leave behind albums that will stand the test of time, rather than just having another hit single. There's a phrase you hear a lot in Nashville, that you're only three and a half minutes away from glory, and I think that's

"He's striving really hard to leave behind albums that will stand the test of time, rather than just having another hit single."
—Scott Siman

"I think that *not* knowing the rules

bullshit. You think you're three and a half minutes away from glory, but the truth is that you're three and a half minutes from becoming a footnote. It's more important to realize that you're forty-five minutes away from a great album that will touch people and make an impact on their lives.

I guess I've always felt like an underdog, and I've always been strong-willed and stubborn about my music. Part of that comes from how I began. I learned to play music in college but I never knew the other side of it—being in the studio and the music business and stuff

like that. Then all of a sudden I was in Nashville and right in the middle of it. I think that not knowing the rules has probably been my biggest blessing. If I had known the rules, I probably wouldn't have been able to do a lot of the things that I've done or made some of the records that I made. I think that not knowing the rules allowed me to find my own style and my own way of doing things that works for me.

When I was growing up in Louisiana, I guess I dreamed of being a rock star as much as any kid does, but I never really pursued music seriously. I was

has probably been my biggest blessing."

into sports, playing baseball, basketball, and football, and that was pretty much my main focus. There were a few times in high school where I tried to start a band or took music lessons or sat down at a piano and tried to write songs, but I never stuck with it. I loved all kinds of music. I'd drive around in my truck listening to the Eagles and Cream and Rush. At the same time, I was a huge fan of George Strait and Alabama and Hank Jr. I think I was lucky that the part of Louisiana where I'm from has a rich musical culture, between the Ozark mountain music and the Mississippi delta music and the East Texas country music and zydeco and all that stuff.

I started to get more serious about music when I was about nineteen. I was in college and not doing too well. I did great in high school and got a scholarship, but as a lot of kids find out, you don't hold up in college as well as you thought you would. I had been in college for a couple of years and was having a great time, but I just knew it wasn't going to work out for me to get a degree, so one summer I bought a guitar. I was living in a house with a bunch of guys and they were all gone, and I had a job where I worked in the mornings so I was just kind of sittin' around. I started listening to records and songs I liked, and started teaching myself to play. By the end of that summer I was playing in some clubs and restaurants for tips, just me and the guitar. At that point, I kind of just closed the book on anything else that I wanted to do, and that was it.

That's when it really hit me; that's when it became "I've gotta do this." It wasn't about becoming a big star; it was more like "Wow, I'm really having a great time, if I could just get a house gig in some bar somewhere, maybe I could make a living doing this." I was so broke that I was just happy to be making a little bit of money. And as I continued doing it, I just fell in love with it more and more and got better and better at it and had more and more confidence. My family and friends all encouraged me to move to Nashville and give it a shot, and that's when I really started thinking "Hey, this is something I might be able to do." And once I made up my mind to do it, it felt like there wasn't any other choice for me. I sold everything I had and went to Nashville, where I didn't know anybody. I think I had about 3000 dollars when I first got to town, and went through most of that the first month and a half.

I think that the only way to succeed is to be completely focused and single-minded about it. If you're going to take the step of doing it, you have to take it all the way. You can't play at it. When you start out, you have to be completely absorbed in what you're doing. It's tough for relationships. I just don't see how anybody who's starting a musical career can make a relationship work. My marriage and family are the best things in my life, but I think I'm lucky that they happened after both my wife and I had had three or four years of success. I think it just made everything blossom.

But I'll admit that there were a lot of sleepless nights during my first couple of years in Nashville. After you start out so confident and it hasn't happened yet, you're laying there thinking, "What am I gonna do with my life? What if this doesn't work out? Is there anything else I can do?"

Byron Gallimore, producer: When Tim came to Nashville, I don't think he was thinking about becoming famous or making a lot of money. I think he came here like all the rest of us, because he loved music. We all gravitate to what we love, and that's what it was with him. He came to Nashville and he just happened to have this wonderful voice, and people noticed.

Scott Siman: In music, you can fabricate stuff or artificially prop it up for a short period, but eventually the fans are going to figure out if you're faking it. The only way that listeners are going to buy into it is if there is a sincerity and a believability and some emotional depth. I think Tim has shared a lot of himself with his fans over the years, and they've come to have

"**He came to Nashville and he just happened to have this wonderful voice, and people noticed.**"
—**Byron Gallimore**

a connection beyond the tunes being catchy or that he's a nice-looking guy. So he's got this really active fan base that looks forward to the next show and the next record, and are interested to see what's he doing and what's he thinking and what he's got up his sleeve. Tim is incredibly in tune with his fans; it's easy for an artist to say, "Oh yeah, I make music for my fans" because that's what they're supposed to say, but Tim actually *does.* When Tim says it, he's telling the truth, because he *is* a fan. He buys other people's records, he goes to other people's shows, and he wants to be moved by music. And so he brings that sensibility to whatever he does. It's true that when you get to his level of success, that gives you total artistic freedom. But with that freedom comes responsibility, and I think he's brilliant at balancing those two things.

Byron Gallimore: When I first met Tim, I went to see him in a little club in downtown Nashville and remember walking out excited but thinking that I wouldn't get to work with him. Later he told me that he liked me a lot from day one and that he decided he wanted to work with me based on personal things,

rather than really knowing what my qualifications were. Tim's very instinctive; he'll get an idea and he'll just go for it. He's not afraid to jump in over his head without a life jacket to see if he can swim—and most of the time, he can. He goes for things, and sometimes maybe he doesn't think about things as much as he should. But it always seems to work for him, so it's hard to argue with that.

I was kind of disappointed in my first album, Tim McGraw; *it sounded good and had some good songs, but I just wasn't as confident or as forceful as I needed to be in picking the songs and getting it to sound the way I wanted it. I wanted to record "Indian Outlaw" for that album, because we'd been doing it live for a few years and the crowds always loved it, but nobody wanted me to cut it.*

When we started cutting Not a Moment Too Soon, *I made up my mind to do it my own way. I had to flip a switch that made me stand up for myself and stand up for what I wanted. I knew it might be my last chance and I had to go for it. That's hard when you're still a new artist without a lot of clout, but I needed to take charge and lay out a path of what I knew I had to*

...I needed
to take
charge
and lay
out a path
of what
I knew
I had to
do in order
to succeed.

do in order to succeed. I'm not so closed-minded that I won't listen to other people's opinions, but I realized that I had to go down my own road or it just wouldn't work for me.

Darran Smith: I think that Tim's always been the kind of guy who just kind of does what he thinks he should do, but I think that the whole thing with the first album and "Indian Outlaw" was definitely a turning point for him. I think it got him to listen to himself and realize that he needed to be himself, instead of trying to be whoever's hot right now. And I think when he recorded his second, *Not a Moment Too Soon,* that's really when he came into his own and

became the artist he was always meant to be.

A great thing that happened as a result of that first album not going anywhere: the record company really wasn't that interested anymore. They were kind of throwing me a bone by letting me make a second album, so I was pretty much left alone with Byron and James Stroud to do what we wanted. So this time I insisted that we were going to record "Indian Outlaw," because I knew it was a hit. And because it was a hit and the album sold six million copies, they continued to leave us alone because I guess they didn't want to mess with a good thing.

"Tim is incredibly in tune with his fans; it's easy

for an artist to say, 'Oh yeah, I make music

for my fans' because that's what they're

supposed to say, but Tim actually *does*."

—**Scott Siman**

"In music, you can fabricate stuff or artificially prop it up for a short period, but eventually the fans are going to figure out if you're faking it." —Scott Siman

the music

WHO ARE THEY?

Maybe it's an obvious thing to say,

but songs are the most important thing that a singer can have.

It doesn't matter who you are or how successful you are, you're nowhere if you don't have a great song. And when you're somebody like me who doesn't generally write his own songs, it's especially important to find the right ones. You need to find songs that feel honest to you, songs that you just feel comfortable singing without feeling like you're hiding behind somebody else's words.

I can't cut a song if it doesn't sound like me, and I've passed on a lot of good songs that have become hit records for other people because of that. It has to be something that makes me think, yeah, I would feel that way in that situation and I would express it that way. Because no matter how good a song is, if it doesn't feel real to you, it's not going to sound real to other people.

You know, I like to cheese out just as much as anybody and do a no-brainer fun song, and there's nothing wrong with that. When I run across a song like that, one that gets me excited, I'll cut it. I like to do serious songs, but I don't like to get so deep and serious that it's like you're trying to *prove* that you're deep and serious. It just has to be something that feels right.

There are a lot of different things that can make a song special; sometimes it's the words, sometimes it's a hook, sometimes it's a groove, sometimes it's a guitar sound. The real magic is when everything comes together—and songs like that don't come along very often. There are some songs that are real simple lyrically, but the coolness of the melody make the lyrics work, or the melody isn't so hot but the lyrics are so powerful that everything falls together. The best scenario is to find a song where everything works, and with this album, I think that all of the songs are like that. The lyrics, the instrumentation, the melody, the licks, the mixes, the harmonies—it all just lays in there great.

When I'm choosing songs for
an album, we always listen to a
lot of songs. I have a team of
people whose ears I trust—
Byron, his wife Missi, the people
in my management office—to
help me find songs that feel
right. In pretty much everything I
do, I tend to go with my gut
instinct, and that's how it is when
I'm looking for songs to cut. I
usually try to stick with my first
instinct because I trust that—or
I've *learned* to trust it, anyway.
That's also the way I approach

"Tim knows hit songs,

and on the rare occasion that he passes on a hit song, he'll say, 'I know that's a hit, but I feel like I've already done that and I don't want to repeat myself.'"

—Byron Gallimore

After

we settled in on 22, 23, 24 songs as possibilities for the album, we played them for the guys and started learning them, and working on getting the **essence of the song.**

Scott Siman: I think if you canvased the Nashville community and asked who's the best artist at picking material, it would be Tim McGraw, hands down. I don't think the competition would even be close. Sometimes you'll play him a song and he'll go, "That's a great song, but it's not a great song for me. I don't hear myself singing that ten years from now." And every once in a while he'll call me and go, "Have a listen to this song, it's not right for me but I think it might be great for one of your other acts, maybe for Billy Gilman or Jessica Andrews." How many artists do *that*?

John Marcus: Tim's got this innate song radar. He can hear a song once and know right away if it's right for him. Even when he hears a demo that's radically different from the way that the actual final product sounds, it's finished in his head before it even gets started.

Byron Gallimore: Tim knows hit songs, and on the rare occasion that he passes on a hit song, he'll say, "I know that's a hit, but I feel like I've already done that and I don't want to repeat myself." I think that everything Tim does comes from a place deep inside of him, and if he doesn't feel it, he can't sing it. I think you can hear that in his delivery on the ballads; he really knows how to connect and how to sell the emotion of a song.

Darran Smith: Yeah, there are songs that Tim actually went and cut that I thought were really great songs, and the next thing you know he passes on them and they become hits for other people. But that doesn't seem to bother him; he'll say, "I'm happy that it worked for him, but it just wasn't for me."

Mark Hurt: One of Kenny Chesney's biggest hits was a song called "How Forever Feels." Tim actually cut that song first, had it mixed, had it finished, and everybody knew it was a stone-cold smash. Everybody around him argued with him about including that song on *Set This Circus Down,* and Tim adamantly refused. His position was, "You guys are right, it's an absolute radio monster hit. But it's not what I want to say, it's not where I am trying to go with my message." This is Tim's art, and when he sings a song he has to feel like it's something he can honestly say. I think that Tim looks at lyrics from the perspective of "Could I sit across the table and say this to somebody?" Tim's gotten to a point in his life and career where he's earned the right to take these chances and step outside the lines. And if it takes four minutes instead of three minutes to deliver the message, then so be it.

"**Tim brought us the demos,** we listened to them once, and then he basically turned us loose to come up with the arrangements. Everybody's ideas are represented in the end result."

—Denny Hemingson

Robert Allen, road manager: Every song that Tim sings relates in some way to his own experience, so that when he sings it he's able to give you that conviction. I think that Tim is fascinated by the fact that songwriters can basically take an entire lifetime and encapsulate it in three and a half minutes, or they can take a second and expand it to three and a half minutes, and he sees it as a challenge to go find those gems. It's amazing; we always laugh about the fact that he can take a stack of 200 CDs that have been picked over and rejected by every other artist in Nashville and find an album's worth of songs.

Julian King, engineer: Maybe I shouldn't say this, but back when we cut "Indian Outlaw," I didn't know why we were even spending the time doing it. But after the fact, he was right. I've never been so happy to be wrong about something! He always manages to see and know his audience. And maybe it's not the shortest road to get to them, but he knows the road.

The whole "Indian Outlaw" thing was definitely a turning point for me, as far as getting comfortable making decisions and sticking with them, and not second-guessing myself. Ever since Not a Moment Too Soon, *we've kind of kept everything in-*

house when I make a record. My label never hears anything until we're done.

A lot of my best songs have come from people's second and third drawers, or from demos that I heard four or five years before that I've remembered. I don't necessarily go after the songs from the top writers in town that everybody else is pursuing, although I do occasionally do some of those too.

I couldn't even tell you who wrote a lot of the songs on the new record, because I don't pay much attention to that. I just listen to the demo twice, decide that I'm cutting the song, and never hear it again until we make the record. I'll walk in kind of halfway knowing it, because that makes the song more immediate because I just don't learn it exactly like it's supposed to be done. I probably piss writers off by changing melodies and stuff, but that's not something that I do on purpose, that's the way it comes out of me. I just run with it.

We listened to a ton of songs for the new record; we always do, but we put in a lot of extra energy this time. We picked a bunch of songs I would have picked under any circumstances, but there are others that were chosen specifically because of what I knew the band would bring to them.

After we settled in on 22, 23, 24 songs as possibilities for the album, we played them for the guys and started learning them, and working on getting the essence of the song. Then we threw the demos away and spent eight weeks in our rehearsal warehouse in Nashville, nine to five Monday through Friday and sometimes weekends, just poring over these songs, learning them inside and out, working out arrangements and experimenting with sounds. I think that that process is what really made this record what it turned out to be. It felt like we were really digging our heels in, building something from the ground up, instead of copying someone else's parts or singing along with a studio track.

Darran Smith: We did *a lot* of preproduction. For seven weeks we were focused on nothing but those songs, pulling them apart and putting them back together, trying to figure out which ones would work and coming up with some kind of musical foundation for them. Tim basically gave us the ball and said, "Look, here's the tunes, make them into Tim McGraw songs." And then he'd come in and we'd throw around different stuff and he'd say, "Yeah, that's real cool" or "Let's try it this way." A couple of demos were sung by women,

so we had to figure out how to make them sound like Tim McGraw tunes. It was hard work, but it was a great experience. What we did in the preproduction stage actually wasn't that much different from what we do when we're preparing for a tour and building a show.

Denny Hemingson: Tim brought us the demos, we listened to them once, and then he basically turned us loose to come up with the arrangements. He pretty much let us have free reign, and then if there was something that he wanted he would speak up. Everybody tossed in ideas, and everybody's ideas are represented in the end result.

Scott Siman: I thought that the preproduction thing was a brilliant idea on Tim's part, setting the band up in the warehouse to hash through the songs. Usually, Tim will record the songs and then the band will adapt and arrange the songs to play them on the road, and there's always cool things that come out of that process. But this time the band did that before recording the songs, so the band's input was built into the songs from the start.

Byron Gallimore is one of my best friends, and he's one of the best music guys I've ever known. He's co-produced all of my

TIM McGRAW AND THE DANCEHALL DOCTORS | 77

"**We did a lot of prepro- duction.** For seven weeks we were focused on nothing but those songs, pulling them apart and putting them back together, try- ing to figure out which ones would work and coming up with some kind of musi- cal founda- tion for them."

—**Darran Smith**

records, and he's an essential part of my team. When I told him that I wanted to record with the Dancehall Doctors on this album, he was completely in favor of it. He knows these guys, so he knew what they're capable of.

Byron Gallimore: This is a vision that Tim's had for awhile. I knew that it was going to be a little more work and take a little more time, but I felt like we could pull it off and it would be worth the extra effort. As Tim's producer, it's my job to assume that we can climb any mountain and find a way to make anything work. It really was a big gamble, because if it didn't work Tim would have been on the spot, but the boys played great. I love working with Tim. We're on the same page in a lot of ways; we have similar tastes in songs, which makes it real easy, and we've worked together for so long that it's a very comfortable fit.

For this project, we also shook things up a little by adding a new member to our production team. We asked Darran Smith to co-produce the album with Byron and me, and that turned out to be a smart move. Darran is a great guy and a great musician, and he's been with me for about a dozen years, so it made sense for him to play a major role in this album. Darran's kind

of a quiet, soft-spoken guy, but when he does talk, he makes a lot of sense. He was the perfect guy for the job, and he really came through.

Darran Smith: I remember the first time Tim talked to me about co-producing. We were at this club and he takes me out to the car and I play him this song that Dave Dunkley and I wrote, and Tim says, "I'm going to make you a producer." And I'm like, "Huh? Really? Okay." And he starts talking about points and things like that, and I'm like, "You mean I'm gonna get paid *too?*" Tim has a habit of doing nice things for people who've been loyal to him, but I didn't want to be the token guy where Tim was giving me this because I'd been with him for twelve years. I wanted to really work and be part of it and cut tracks and stuff. He let me work, that's for sure.

Julian King: I'll say that even I was thinking on the first day of cutting, "Where are we going with this?" But Tim's always taken some chances that not everybody expected of him. I was impressed that he took it to a new level and trusted his instincts.

Ricky Cobble, engineer: I've worked on every record after the first two, so I started on *All I Want* as an assistant engineer to Julian. I guess basically I

"**I had fun with those guys and really got to know them better. I worked a lot with Dean and Darran and Denny on guitar overdubs. Byron did a pretty hands-off thing and let them do their thing on overdubs. He'd come in and give direction and leave. We worked all day and he'd be checking in once or twice. A lot of it had to do with the trust he had in those guys.**"

—Erik Lutkins

"**Byron is the best country producer** happening today. He knows what's going to work and he knows how to make it a hit. In the studio, he was like a coach. He'd say, 'I'm not sure that's going to work. Can we come up with a new chord to work in that part right there?'"

—Ricky Cobble

"**Tim's always taken some chances that not everybody saw of him. I was impressed that he took it to a new level and trusted his instincts.**"

—Julian King

still am. On every record I've
engineered some stuff and
pulled a 3 or 4 in the morning
with Byron on the couch. Byron is
the best country producer happening today. He knows what's
going to work and he knows how
to make it a hit. In the studio, he
was like a coach. He'd say, "I'm
not sure that's going to work.
Can we come up with a new
chord to work in that part right
there?" It was a mutual thing—
him and Darran and Tim and the
guys working together. He might
hear something they weren't
hearing and suggest putting
another note in a chord or something like that.

Erik Lutkins, engineer: I
think the band was sort of surprised that they cut as much as
they did. Byron and Tim really
controlled the pace of the whole
session. We wouldn't cut until
after lunch, but we'd be doing
something all the time—overdubs or getting sounds or whatever all through the day. In some
respects, we all weren't expecting the kind of quality we got
from the band. I don't mean that
negatively—it's a positive thing.
The band just did a really great
job. The sounds were great.
John Prestia worked really hard
on the guitar sounds. Joey was
totally on it making sure everything and everyone had what
they needed. It felt like a team
when we got rolling.

"Tim's got

this innate song radar.
He can hear a song once and know right away if it's right for him."

—John Marcus

the place

I always liked that old Rolling Stones/ Led Zeppelin idea of going to a castle in the Swiss Alps or a deserted island to make an album.

So rather than recording in the comfortable, familiar surroundings of Nashville, I wanted to cut this album in a more isolated atmosphere, far from the distractions of home, family, friends, and the music business.

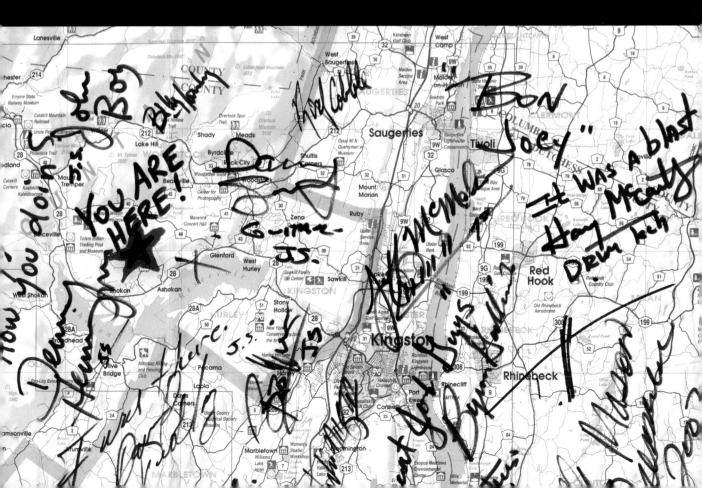

Robert Allen: Tim said to me, "You need to go to Ireland to find a castle in the country for us to record in." My research took me across the entire globe, trying to find what

he was looking for. Fortunately, a studio referral company turned me on to Allaire, and we got on a plane and flew up to see the studio.

After searching around for awhile, we settled on Allaire Studio, near Woodstock in upstate New York. The studio is located in a beautiful old farmhouse on top of a

mountain in the Catskills, and it's loaded with vintage instruments and analog recording gear, which tied in with my goal of getting a warm, organic sound. I've always been a fan of that approach, so finding Allaire was like a dream come true.

"It wasn't perfect by any stretch of the imagination, and technically it took a lot to pull it off, but we managed to make it work. I hired an ambience person and a technical person that I took with me just to make sure that it looked the way Tim wanted it to look, felt the way he wanted it to feel, and sounded the way he expected it to sound. I enlisted my entire road crew; none of us had never been involved with the recording process in the past, but the crew was instrumental in getting the project done."

—Robert Allen

John Ward, front-of-house sound engineer: We didn't want to be stuck up there and find that we were missing something, so we brought everything that we could possibly bring.

Joey (Bon Joey) Supak, drum tech: We had a fifty-three-foot semi full of gear, front to back, top to bottom. We brought up ten or fifteen amplifiers, five or six drum kits, and sixty or seventy guitars, on top of whatever was in-house at the studio. John Prestia and I were the first ones to arrive, which is a story in itself. Everything was late, we got lost, and then when we finally got there we got snowed in.

John Prestia, guitar tech: We couldn't drive the truck up the mountain, so we had to offload it down at the bottom of the mountain and make a bunch of trips up with a smaller truck. It took a day just to get the gear up the mountain, but once we got in there and got everything set up, it worked out really well. We brought in a lot of vintage amps and a ton of guitars, and put a lot of work into getting cool guitar sounds.

One of the reasons we picked Allaire was because they had the old Neve console and an old two-inch tape machine. And up in their attic, they had about 150 vintage guitars, 200 vintage amps, and something like sixty old vintage keyboards. It was great having all that stuff around to play with. We'd plug in all kinds of things and try them—fiddles through guitar amps, you name it—and ended up keeping a lot of it.

Working in the studio can get a little stale, and for this project we wanted to create a comfortable atmosphere that would encourage creativity and inspiration. So we brought in an ambience guy who decorated the studio to create the right vibe, and that made a big difference.

10:32 on the 6th of March.
      Damn guitars take a long time!
working on "I don't want to go to sleep
tonight" and still working on guitar
sounds and I just gotta say, if
I don't the shower in the room doesn't
get me the the catering will.
      The shower floor is slippery as a mo fo!
and the food here is exceptional

at ease maybe I can calm down and just
play! Tim really digs whats going on - a
a good sign. I missed my run today
... damn video game! Gotta go
working on I want the best.

AFTER dinner We Cut Ticking Away — real fast
and also cut / She brings the lightning down.
We have all been racing this car game. 4 people
at a time, loser moves ...

Day 4 march 7

We gonna Have Ribs tonight.
Ribs Are good. Cut Lightning.
Things on the verge of out of
Control. Probably good to blow
off steam. Getting great stuff.

Dean Brown: I never saw the place prior to the decorator coming in, but the people who worked there were amazed by the transformation—Oriental rugs and candles everywhere, and all of the bedrooms had different motifs. There were pens and writing tablets everywhere, in case we had an idea and wanted to write it down. Tim brought in some Sega racing games, so whenever we weren't recording or eating, we were racing. We were up at the top of this mountain, in an old chalet with huge stone fireplaces and a great big bar, and surrounded by forest. You could wake up, walk out of your room, stumble in and grab some coffee, walk across a little grassy courtyard, and you're in the studio. You couldn't really get in or out, because it was ten miles down that mountain on narrow, winding roads, so if we needed something we had to send somebody down to get it for us.

We wanted to make the experience perfect for the guys and I also wanted to make sure that we captured all of it. So we rounded up four different cameras and all kinds of different film. I wanted black and white and color; different speeds for different looks and lighting. We had the cameras just sitting out so that everyone could shoot. All of the pictures from the studio were taken either by me or by someone else who was there. We also had Sherman Halsey come in and film as much as he could. Sherman has done all of my videos and has been around with all of us for years—so it made sense for him to be there.

Mamsies Cooking & Baking Co.

Dinner
March 6, 2002
Asian Glazed Salmon
Steamed Brocolli
Rice Medley

Saugerties, NY 12477   (914) 246-9367

Sherman Halsey, director/producer: The trick is that you don't want to intrude on the recording process—which is all about getting the mood right—but at the same time you need a little light to shoot. So we lit the room before Tim got there, and of course, he felt like it was too much. We're always playing that game where I'm trying to sneak in more light and he's wanting it darker and moodier. So we turned it off—and snuck more candles in to try and get it lit that way. I think it ended up being better because the extra candlelight just added to the overall ambience.

Kelly Wright, senior vp creative, rpm management: Tim requested that each guy have a gift bag sitting in his room when he arrived at the studio. He wanted everything from sweats to a DVD player to a cool journal they could write in and keep notes or doodle pictures. He thought of

everything. He had given a list to Robert and the two of us went out and rounded up the contents. By the time we were done, it wouldn't fit in the bags we bought, so it ended up being a gift *box.* The bus came by the office on the Saturday before they left, so that we could load them into the bays without the guys knowing or seeing anything. I felt like we were sending the kids off to camp.

Darran Smith: Tim did just about everything you can imagine to make it a relaxing, laid-back atmosphere. He really went above and beyond trying to take some of the pressure off of us, so we could be comfortable enough to just play. That was good, because when you're not intimidated or nervous you can just play what you feel. If there was any nervousness, I think it was in trying to make Byron happy. But he was upbeat and did his best to make us feel comfortable. *While we were at Allaire, we stayed in this beautiful old house, ate incredible meals that the chefs prepared, and enjoyed the amazing views of the mountains. But mainly it was about making music, and being up on this mountain far away from everybody else allowed us to focus on the job we were there to do. We could have done it in a formal studio*

"Tim did just about every-thing you can imagine to make it a relax-ing, laid-back atmosphere."
—Darran Smith

Denny-

Welcome to Allaire Studios.

Your long distance account code is: **365**

The front gate code for your project is: **#1930**

All information on operating the phone system is in the black Allaire Studios Welcome Kit located near the telephone. For your convenience, your outgoing voicemail message has already been recorded for you.

If you have forgotten anything (i.e. toothbrush, razor and shaving cream, etc.) or are in need of anything (i.e. more towels, aspirin, etc.) ask any Allaire staff member. They will do their best to keep you as comfortable as possible.

Thank you for working here at Allaire Studios. We hope your stay is a pleasant one.

#1930 GATE CODE

Tim ARRIVES

RIFFON A

Contact Name: K

I 87 →

Follow Si

Prive to A

2 blocks o

Go to GA

E.

8 8 - 3

in Nashville and showed up every morning and gone home every night, but it wouldn't have been the same. It was all about recreating the vibe we have on the bus when we're out playing every night, but instead of the bus we were all in a great room with a fireplace, playing until four o'clock in the morning trying to get the song right.

Kelly Wright: Tim and Faith have a "rule" that has been fairly well publicized that they don't stay apart from each other for more than three days in a row. I was in the room when Darran gave out the emergency number to the studio and told the band that they needed to talk to their significant others and get it straight that they weren't going to be able to call home all the time or have a bunch of incoming calls. He was clear that this was serious business. This was about four days before they left and you could feel the mix of anxiety and excitement in these guys. He finished the conversation by saying, "Tim's breaking the three-day rule himself. So this is a pretty big deal." And you could totally feel the room take that in. We all know the significance of the three-day rule and how important it is to both Tim and Faith. This was a huge statement that they both knew how much this meant to Tim personally, not just professionally.

I loved the focus we had there, because there were no distractions. Everything was about cutting the record. It was like being in a submarine and not having time to think about anything other than our mission. Our whole universe was making that record in that place. We're there and the fire is going and the song is great and everybody's playing great and everybody's feeling great and we're locking in on something that sounds good. In that moment, when everything's going great and the music's flowing, you forget how long you've been there and how long you're going to be there. It was the most fulfilling and enjoyable experience I've ever had recording, and I want to do the same thing on our next album. I'm sure I'll do other kinds of records again somewhere down the line, but it sure would be hard to give up doing something that's this much fun.

6:00 pm. 3/4/02
    Not sure what time we arrived but we were forced to hang on the bus until they picked us up. The drive up the mountain was Spectacular..!!

The Studio is very ... comfy! 1800 style decor with miles & miles of space beauty, the mountains are awesome..!!

Tim as always, took care of his brothers with some mighty nifty gift bags/boxes, complete with portable DVD player! holy sheep shit! cool sweats kitchen shoes unbelievable! This is going to be an incredible journey.

"Being at the studio put us in that alien environment."

—Julian King

Julian King: Being at the studio put us in that alien environment. It was like a science project for everybody—so it made us really get outside our everyday worlds. None of us were worried about getting the kids to soccer practice. We were presented with technical issues that were challenging and as a result, we got some really interesting sounds. We were sleeping and drinking Tim McGraw and this music. It wasn't just some ego thing— "Tim"—it was a big team up on the hill.

Sunday Early Evening we
are Starting on Illegal.

The Snow has started, you cant
See off the mountain.....

(I hope it Covers)

It was all about re-creating the vibe we have on the bus when we're out playing every night, but **instead of the bus we were all in a great room with a fireplace, playing until four o'clock** in the morning trying to get the song right.

the record

Recording is a tricky process, because you're working really hard and using all this technology to try and create something that sounds like you're not trying. You can't just open the mike and play because it's not going to automatically come out sounding like what you sound like; you've got to get all the pieces to work together so it hits the tape right. You want it spontaneous and real, but you also want it to sound good. It was a lot of work to get it all to sound right, because we had to piece a lot of stuff together, and the drum room had to be 100 yards away, so we had to run cables out in the snow. The situation presented a lot of technical challenges, but I think the challenges kind of made it more exciting.

"It was like you could feel that the weight had lifted, and any apprehension or nervousness had totally gone away."

—Julian King

Julian King: I've worked with Tim on every album and I could tell that he was pretty nervous when he first got there. He was pacing a lot and up and standing. But on the second day, after we had a few tracks behind us, I looked over and he was sneaking in a catnap on the couch. We were just doing busy work stuff—plugging stuff in and getting things right. It was great to see that he had relaxed enough to fall asleep. It was, like, you could feel that the weight had lifted, and any apprehension or nervousness had totally gone away.

Darran Smith: The main tracking room was the house's old dining room, which was a big room with a huge fireplace, over-looking the mountain. It was great; you had anything you could want right there, so we'd just sit and cut and do it how-ever many times we needed to do it. No pressure, just play it the best you can and move on. We cut like in the old days, when they used to all get in the one big room, and the control room was right in the room. We had partitions up to isolate the instruments, and Billy was way across the compound.

John Marcus: We had peo-ple scattered all over the build-ing, playing in different rooms, and Billy was in another build-ing. They ran like a 500-foot snake over to the other building and he was all alone. That was kind of weird for me, because I'm used to standing next to the drummer and having eye contact with him. We had TV monitors that were split four ways so you could see everybody else. I'm used to staring Billy in the face when we play, so it was weird to try and lock in with a tiny image on a TV screen.

Billy Mason: It was hard to be over there alone. When we'd cut tracks, I could see Byron talking on the monitor but I couldn't hear him, I was freaking out because there'd be times when I'd just sit there for

"We had people scattered all over
the building, playing in different rooms."
—John Marcus

"I set it up on Denny's steel so he could see the other guys **on the monitor behind him.**"

—John Prestia

fifteen or twenty minutes and not hear a word. I'd be wondering if I sucked, while they talked between themselves. I'd count off the songs really loud because I was stuck there all alone and I needed to scream to create some energy for myself. It was dark and it's this old medieval-looking house, and people have told me that it's haunted, so while I was waiting alone and not knowing what the hell was going on, I'd have weird thoughts—"If a ghost got me, they'd never know what happened . . ."

John Prestia: I felt bad for Denny, because he was set up with the TV to his back. I thought it would be nice if he could see those guys. I found a car rearview mirror laying out in the driveway, so I set it up on Denny's steel so he could see the other guys on the monitor behind him.
We definitely established a certain comfort level by getting out of Nashville and not having friends and record-company people stopping by. I wanted our comfort level to be so high that everybody would feel comfortable voicing

their opinion and trying things and not being afraid of messing up. I think that the guys might have felt some pressure at first until everybody started playing and the atmosphere got going.

Ricky Cobble: Tim just brought this vibe in that made everybody feel comfortable, at home, laid back. That made it really different than coming in and working on the clock and going home. It was like all those records you hear about where people get to go in and cut and not worry about the time. Technically, it was also really different. There was no control room really. The console was in this big room that was all decorated and everybody—the producer, the engineers, the guys—were all in the same room. That created a vibe right there. The drums and a couple booths were outside the main room but they had TV monitors so they could still be a part of it. That's just not done much these days. Like if you listen to "Red Ragtop"—which is my favorite—there's something really special that came out of cut-

at ease maybe I can calm down and jus'
play. Tim really digs what's going on. a
a good sign. I missed my run today
... damn video game! Gotta go
working on. I want the best.

12:20 am

ting it the way we did—with everyone together. I can't tell you why, but it was just Tim and the way the guys played—it just made the song. It was organic.

Darran Smith: In the past, I've sat in the studio and watched Tim cut stuff with the studio players. Those guys do that every day and they've got their formula down and it's not like Tim can look at them and go, "Man, that sucked, can we try something else?" I think that working with us gave him more control, because with us, he can feel comfortable saying, "Aw, that was shit, you can do better than that."

David Dunkley: I think everyone felt a little intimidated going into this project. We all had certain doubts and insecurities, and we all had to talk each other through it and pep-talk each other to believe that we could pull this off. And over and over again, we just kept comin' through and doing what we do. I don't think we all got completely comfortable until we got to the studio and surpassed what we were expected to come up with.

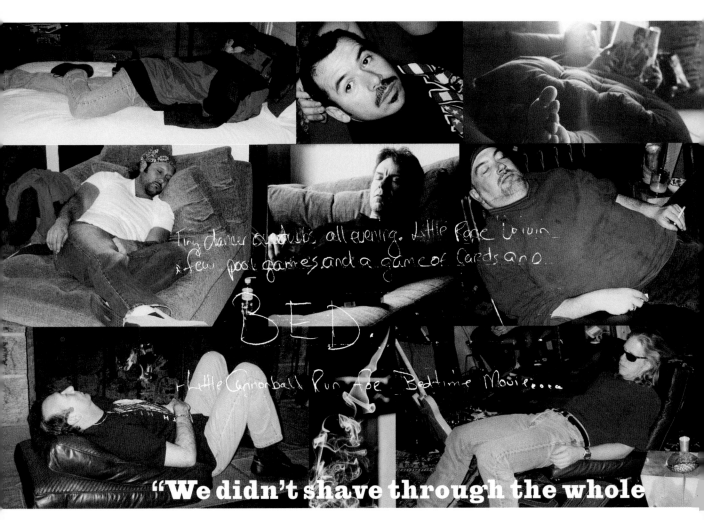

Tiny dancer conducts all evening. Little Pete drivin a few pool games and a game of cards and... BED.

+ Little Cannonball Run Joe Bedtime Movie....

"We didn't shave through the whole session. It's that old baseball thing, when you're on a winning streak and you can't shave until you lose a game."

—Jeff McMahon

Darran Smith: We recorded at Allaire for eleven days, and the expectations were for us to get maybe six basic tracks. We walked down the mountain with seventeen. Everybody was pretty surprised about that. So were we.

Jeff McMahon: We didn't shave through the whole session. It's that old baseball thing, when you're on a winning streak and you can't shave until you lose a game.

Darran Smith: We had running jokes about the studio cats waiting on call at the airport. In fact, we invented a board game; every time one of us screwed up, the studio guy gets another jump forward. And if you come up with a really good part, then he goes home and unpacks his bag.

John Prestia: I can see why the situation might have been somewhat intimidating for the guys in the band, because Tim's breaking the Nashville rules and people are looking to the band to come up with the goods. I think that a little bit of fear can be a good thing in the studio. It keeps you on edge and keeps you from getting too comfortable. The guys did great, and it was cool to see them get a chance to shine. It was loose, but at the same time there was a definite discipline. Tim even invited me to play on a couple of songs; I got to play guitar on "Sing Me Home" and harmonica on "Who Are They?" which was pretty cool.

Byron Gallimore: It was a little more time-consuming working with a real band rather than Nashville session players.

But the beauty of doing the album this way is that these guys are digging in and every moment means something. They're busting it every moment and giving it everything they got, and that comes through in the music.

Darran Smith: It was cool working with Byron. He didn't say anything for awhile about me coproducing, and I started wondering if Tim had just been screwing with me. My first acknowledgment from Byron was when I came in while Jeff was cutting keyboards, and Byron goes, "I gotta go over here and do something with Dean. Why don't you go ahead and cut Jeff here on these tracks?" I was like, "Really, Dad, I can drive?" After that, he was really good about letting me take charge and run with stuff; he trusted me enough to not feel like he had to be there every minute. That was also good because I'm forty-two years old, and I

can't see me jumping around in leather pants out there when I'm fifty-something. I'm building a studio at my house and trying to get into producing other acts, so this was a nice push in that direction.

I don't know if Tim's got the patience to sit and become a serious, disciplined musician, but he's got a great ability to tell you what he hears in a way

that you know almost off the bat what he's talking about. At one point in the studio he said, "Make this more humid— not hotter, but more humid," and you go, "Okay." At first, it might not make any sense, but you'll play it and try different things and realize, "Oh, that's what he means."

Making this record was

> **"It kind of brought you back to that feeling that you had when you first discovered music— when you'd get a group of people together and jam in somebody's garage."**

the most fun I've ever had in a recording studio and the most fun I've ever had with all of us together. We've been playing music together for all this time, and now we finally had this

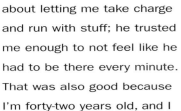

great opportunity to hang out in this great place for fifteen days with great equipment and great songs, and get a great record out of it. It was kind of a frathouse atmosphere; you're with your buddies and interacting and drawing on all of the history and chemistry you've got. It kind of brought you back to that feeling that you had when you first discovered music— when you'd get a group of people together and jam in somebody's garage or somebody's bedroom until three or four in the morning.

It just felt like we were diving in and rolling our sleeves up and getting our hands dirty. Not that I haven't been involved in my records before, but when you're making a record the typical way, there can be an element of punching a time clock. And I'm sure I'll do that again, but for this project it just felt like we owned it, from the first note to the last. It feels like "Yeah, this is ours."

After our time at Allaire was up, we brought the tapes back to Nashville, where we cut three more songs and did some additional overdubbing of instruments on the tracks we'd cut at Allaire. We did that stuff in a more conventional studio atmosphere, but I think we brought a lot of the loose, organic vibe back with us from Allaire, so the work we did in Nashville felt like an extension

of what we'd been doing.

Darran Smith: When me and Denny went in and cut eight or nine days of guitar overdubs, Tim and Byron pretty much turned it over to us; I think we saw Byron maybe twice the whole time. It was kind of cool but it was kind of weird too, because you're standing in this room, that's like you're standing in like a 2,500-dollar-a-day studio that's just you in this big room by yourself and you're kind of looking around going, all this for me? We were making these executive decisions on the fly, and finally at the end of that Byron says, "I hope you guys didn't think I was blowing you off, but I didn't want to come in there and break up your vibe." That made us feel pretty good.

Dean Brown: We did the overdubs in a regular audio studio—no incense, no candles— so I would just try and remember how it felt at the time we cut the track and I just pictured that room and the view of the mountain, and that kind of brought it back.

Darran Smith: Even in the mixes, Tim was going for the more raw, soulful thing. He would get mixes back and he'd say, "That's too vanilla-sounding" or "That's too smooth" or "That's too slick." He wanted it good and tight but not slick. When I finally got the final mix on everything, I went home and

"Tim's always referring to the album as having an earthy vibe to it and saying how **you can hear the sweat on the strings."**

—Dean Brown

sat down with a couple of Tim's early albums and *Set This Circus Down* and went back and forth between those and the new one. It's definitely a Tim McGraw record—you know that right off the bat when you hear it—but it's a little more raw, it's a little more rockin' and a lot more soulful. It doesn't sound like a Nashville record, it sounds more like what they used to cut down in Muscle Shoals in the '60s and '70s. But the tunes still sound like hit country radio songs. One of the best feelings was when Tim came back with the mix of "My Kind of Rain" and he was really excited about it and said, "Byron says he thinks this is the best record that either he or I has ever done."

Dean Brown: Tim's always referring to the album as having an earthy vibe to it and saying how you can hear the sweat on the strings, and I'd agree with that.

David Dunkley: It's got heart and guts; you can tell we've all got blood, sweat, and tears invested in this thing.

Robert Allen: The new material also has some of the best singing that Tim's done,

and I think that came out of the environment that we created. We basically took the environment that we have on the road and recreated it in the studio, which is the only way I ever knew to record before I came to Nashville.

Scott Siman: I think that Tim would say that this music is as close as he's ever come to making the record that he's always heard in his head. I think that *A Place in the Sun* and *Set This Circus Down* have some of that vision, but maybe they didn't get all the way there. It's not an easy task to make that happen; it's a hard thing to get musicans and producers and engineers and mastering people and management people and record company people on that same train long enough to make something like that happen. *I definitely feel like this record is way more me than any record I've ever done. I've always been very involved in making my records, but this one feels like more than just another record. I just think it's in a completely different league; it's just kinda leaps and bounds, and the whole thing has taken on a whole new life for me. It's got a lot of sweat and heart and soul, and the guys just played their asses off. I think that I sang more honestly on this record, and I think that came from the honesty that the music was*

Day 7 march 10

After much racing and
really good food, basic
tracks are 1 from finished.
The boyz did good.

played with. It's not like my other records haven't been honest, but on these tracks it felt like I could just jump in and feel the songs, because there's some sweat on the strings.

What I love about this record is that everybody's performing and giving it everything they've got, and it feels real because of that. It's real earthy and organic and it sounds like a bunch of guys who've known each other and lived together for a really long time and really enjoy playing music together. And you can't make a record like that unless you've invested the time to build that kind of chemistry.

As much as we wanted to make a different kind of record, we weren't looking to alienate our fans. I think that the music business likes to create a mystique about what it takes to make a commercial-sounding record, but I don't agree with that. I believe that when people listen to music, they listen with their hearts, and what they're really listening for is a good song and an honest performance. And if

you give them that, the chances are that you're going to get through.

It's hard for me to pick a favorite song from this record because I love all of them. "She's My Kind of Rain" might be my favorite thing that I've done so far; that was one that I could really sink my teeth into and feel good about singing. But all of the new songs were fun to sing. "Red Ragtop" is another favorite of mine; I think it's just one of those lyrics that anybody can relate to. Anybody could cut it and it would still be a smash. I really love the simplicity and honesty of "Love You Well." And Faith loves "All We Ever Find"; that's one of her favorites. Having Don Henley and Timothy B. Schmit singing on "Illegal" was a dream come true since the Eagles are one of my all-time favorite bands.

"Illegal" and "Tickin' Away" were songs that I originally recorded with a band called Kattl; I produced them in '96. It was one of my first adventures into producing and we cut some things that I thought were great. They were a great band, but they kind of fell apart and nothing really happened with the stuff we recorded. I kept those songs in the back of my mind, and eventually we started playing them live and made them ours. They were perfect for the band.

March 13, 2002   9:50 A.M. a.T2.

    not believing it's already over
I'm here in my room looking
over the courtyard where our snow
man stares defiantly at the sun.
I wonder if this is one of those events
that will captivate my grandchildren
as I rock them at story time ...?
"I remember the day ... "

the delivery

After we got the record finished, we went back out on the road for a summer 2002 tour, which gave us the chance to preview some of the new songs for the fans. It also gave the guys in the band a chance to play the parts they created in front of people, rather than just replicating other people's licks. I can't tell you how great it felt to be playing the music that we all created together on stage, and the fans' enthusiastic response to the new tunes confirmed that we were right in approaching the album the way we did.

The stages that we play on are bigger now, and the production's more elaborate, but our show isn't all that different from what we were doing when we started out playing in little clubs and honky-tonks. We're pretty much doing the same thing we were doing then with the same kind of energy level, but with bigger lights, better toys, and more people watching.

Darran Smith: We're still like a glorified bar band. We're having fun up there and that's what comes across to the crowd. You might hear a clunker here or a flat note there, but I've never heard anybody come away from a show going, "Oh man, that bum note really wrecked my night." We make plenty of mistakes, but the

"Even early on in the clubs, **Tim has always tried to keep the band involved** as a big part of the show. For as long as I've been with him, it's been an interactive thing." —Bob Minner

crowd never seems to mind as long as the spirit's there and everybody's having fun. As long as Tim's ass is flying, man, they're happy. I mean, God bless him, I don't see it myself, but if you look down at the women in the crowd their eyes are all locked onto that ass like a tractor beam.

John Marcus: The biggest comment I get is "You guys look like you're havin' a blast up there." That kind of thing rubs off on people. The band vibe has always been there from the start, and it's something that Tim has always encouraged. I just think Tim wanted to be able to interact with his buddies and not just have some stiffs standing behind him.

Bob Minner: Even early on in the clubs, Tim has always tried to keep the band involved as a big part of the show. For as long as I've been with him, it's been an interactive thing. Tim's the boss, but he's also one of the guys. He makes you feel involved and that makes a big difference in your attitude toward your work. I think that's part of what makes a good leader. Tim understands that it takes a team of people to execute his vision, and that extends to his relationship with his crew and his management team. You run into a lot of musicians on the road, and they're always amazed that Tim includes us in the tour book or includes us on a T-shirt. For those guys, it's more like "I just work for this guy and he pays me this much and he never talks to me and I don't know if I'll still be here next year." Tim's the boss, and it's his show, but he's also one of us.

Darran Smith: Back in the early days, it felt like we played every honky-tonk, country bar, and dance hall in the country. We were doing something like 300 gigs a year, just pulling in, playing the gig, pulling back out, and going to the next one. That's pretty much all we did for the first couple of years, up until *Not a Moment Too Soon* hit. We had a couple of crew guys and the cheapest bus you could get, and it was hard work, but it was good. I think we always pictured ourselves as underdogs, because when we started out, it felt like we were the only ones who believed in us. On stage, we really played it to the hilt, so by the time we'd leave a club they'd be like, "You guys are the best band we've ever had in here." We *weren't,* but the way we had fun and put that across made it seem like we were. And of course Tim helped a lot on that because he'd get crazy and jump around and jump off risers and stuff. And the more crazy he got, the more crazy we got, and the more crazy the crowd got.

Mark Hurt: Tim's always had that innate star quality. Even in the early days, in a club with 100 people that didn't have any idea who anybody on the stage was, Tim had that knack for grabbing everybody's attention and holding them in the palm of

I don't think anybody really gets us until they see us onstage all playing together at the same time.

his hand and then setting them down gently and leaving everybody going "Damn!" Even when he was just doing cover songs. If you had to come up with a description of what Tim McGraw's all about, you'd really have to go and see a live performance. Tim's a pretty normal, down-to-earth guy in real life, but he walks on that stage and becomes something totally different. Tim grew up as an athlete—he played basketball, baseball, and football through high school and he was all-state a couple of years. And I think that he brings that mentality of "Just throw me the ball" and that whole team spirit to his music. He's comfortable in situations where the pressure is the motivator and you hear 10,000 people screaming and it's an adrenaline rush. I've been watching him do that for years, and it boggles my mind how somebody could do that, like how does a guy go and perform brain surgery?

If you look at us on stage, there's so much diversity and individuality. Everybody's just so different, but when everybody comes together it adds up to something that makes sense. I don't think anybody really gets us until they see us on stage all playing together at the same time. It's completely a team, and I really do depend on these guys to make the music work. In situations where I've had to perform somewhere without the band, like on TV or at an awards show, I'm always a nervous wreck. It feels like I don't have my hands with me or something.

"…the women in the crowd, their eyes are all locked onto that ass like a tractor beam."

I think the main thing that makes this band so cool to be around is just how much we all like each other. There's no ego or attitude, but at the same time there's this underlying pride in what we do. That's a pretty good thing to have, because it really jacks up the energy level when we need it. When we go out on the road, it's kind of like a big frat house on wheels, and we tried to capture some of that feeling on this record. It's not just the playing, it's the bantering and the wise-cracks and the basketball and everything that goes along with it.

Bob Minner: I think that, as much as he's the star, Tim feels more comfortable having a team of guys on stage that he can interact with. I think that that kind of takes some of the pressure off him and makes him feel more comfortable. I think that if people are going to spend their hard-earned money to see our show, they deserve to see eight guys working just as hard as the guy they've come to see.

David Dunkley: I've gotten to see firsthand how a lot of other artists treat their bands and how they treat the people around them, and I've learned from experience that Tim is really a rarity. Tim's not insecure about sharing the spotlight and letting everybody else get some attention. I think a lot of other artists would hate it if one of their guys tried to steal his thunder. But with Tim, if you try to steal his thunder, it just pushes him to work harder. This is a really good band on a few different levels; we play really well together, but we also do good together on the bus. There's a real brotherly kind of vibe, and the kind of comfort level that comes with family. It makes a

big difference when you're on the bus and you can tell someone, "Hey, tonight you really pissed me off" and know that he's not going to hate you in the morning for it. It's weird that it works so well, because we're such a diverse assortment of personalities, and it's amazing that we can all live together in such close quarters and not step on each other's toes.

Billy Mason: It's a cool gig, and it really does feel like Tim and these guys are my brothers. When we're out on the road, we play basketball together, we run together and go to the gym together. Tim's definitely one of the guys, but he still demands perfection, even if it's just basketball.

Denny Hemingson: The same way Tim has an ability to pick songs, he seems to have an ability to pick people he knows will do a good job and people he doesn't have to police all the time. He doesn't really say a lot, he just lets you do your thing, and if something is not going the way he wants, he'll let you know.

Jeff McMahon: Tim isn't the kind of guy to hire somebody and then try to mold him into what he wants him to be. I think everybody knows what his job is but nobody's hung up on what his job is. It's like, the job is to make a record and put on a good show, and everybody's willing to step up and do whatever needs to be done for that to happen. And it's not just the band, it's the crew and the management. Everybody

"It's a cool gig,

and it really does feel like Tim and these guys are my **brothers. When** we're out on the road, we play basketball together, we run together and go to the gym together."

—Billy Mason

is given enough rope to hang himself, and everybody is given the opportunity to rise to the occasion. Which is just good management, because you can get a lot more done if you surround yourself with capable, responsible people and let them do what you hired them to do.

Joey (Bon Joey) Supak: The feeling of being part of a team

definitely extends to the crew, and the new album is a good example of that. It was a lot of work for everybody, but I think that we all felt like we had a stake in the end result. We're all gonna look back at it and show it to our grandkids and say, "Hey, I was part of this project." Tim is wonderful about making people feel like they fit. The joke among the five full-time crew guys is that we're the bastard sons of country music

because we've all had other gigs, but we've all found a home here.

Manny Medieros, ground rigger and set carpenter: Tim's funny because out on tour, he's always around. He's always watching everybody. He knows exactly what he's got there. He knows if something's going wrong. You may not even know he's there. You turn around and he's been watching you for five minutes. Metaphorically, you know, he's the quarterback. He's not going to do all the drills that the linemen do and all that, but he's in the game. He's not just rolling out of the car and onto the stage. He works on his attitude all day long. He's up, walking around, eating, playing ball—working his way to the show—one way or another.

Robert Allen: Tim and Faith are both very family oriented, and that's the feeling that Tim tries to create in his organization. It's nice to try and create an atmosphere where everybody feels like his contribution is significant. There are aspects of the job that can be very monotonous, so the feeling that you're part of something bigger can be what keeps you going on a daily basis.

John Prestia: I've been around, and I've encountered a lot of talented people who are really negative and miserable to be around. Personally, I'd rather try and enjoy life,

and that's the way it is with this group of people.

John Ward: It's business, but it's also family. Most of the people that come on the road with us as independent contractors say they've never been out on a tour where it's been so nice and everybody enjoys doing his job. They're also used to being on eggshells around the star, and that's definitely not the case with Tim. Since the beginning, there's always been a spirit of fun and playfulness, and we've never lost that. And that atmosphere is generated mainly by Tim.

Tom "Zep" Lyster, head rigger: Tim asked me once a long time ago, "How much longer are you going to do this?" And I said, "Until you get to be Entertainer of the Year and then some." I stuck

around for his sense of family. There's never a time that he didn't have a great deal of humility about what he's achieved. Last year at the final show of the year, he called us all around and said, "I want you to know that I didn't win this [CMA Entertainer of the Year] award, we did." There's a certain maturity that develops when you get to start off with somebody. You all grow along together. There's a sincerity that you can't get any other way. It keeps everybody honest—which can be painful. At the end of a five-day run, we can get a little ragged, but if anyone from the outside took a poke at us, we'd rally for each other pretty quickly.

the future

I see this record as a step toward getting on the path that I want to be on musically, making great records as a band and then being able to go out and play the same stuff that we played on the records. There are a lot of different kinds of records I want to make someday, but as far as the foreseeable future, I really like what happened on this album and I want to try to make that happen again. This feels like the direction that I want to go in. I really want to make music that blows people away and defies their expectations, and you can't accomplish that by just going in and making another record

The guys in my band have always played their hearts out on stage, but until now they've always always been playing music that was created by other musicians. But when we play the new songs live now, the vibe is different, because the guys are playing parts they created, rather than other people's parts that they learned off a record. That makes such a difference, because everybody's feeling an emotional investment in these songs, and that ups the ante a little. I think it's also made the old songs feel fresher to everybody, because doing this project made everybody feel so confident that they're digging back into the older stuff and kind of reexamining the way they play it and adding more of their own thing. The whole project has been a big shot of adrenaline into the band, so for me it's already a success.

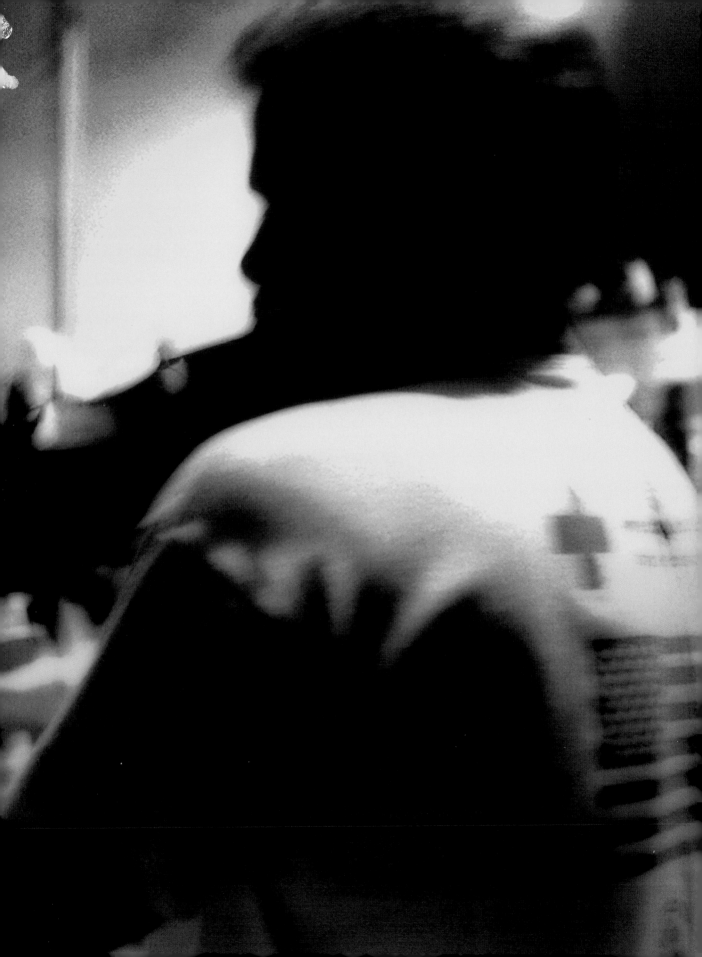

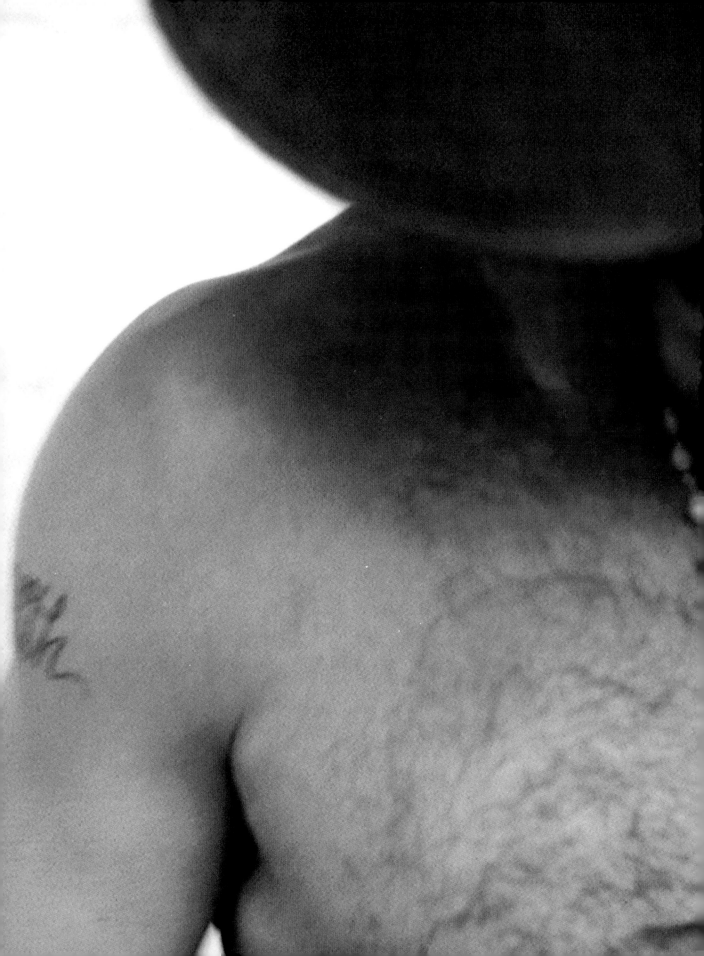

Darran Smith: I think it's definitely given us a new sense of confidence in what we can do. We've been playing other guys' licks for so long that it's great to be playing our own stuff. And that feeling has been carrying over into the older songs. I've played "I Like It, I Love It" a million times, but somehow it feels a little fresher now.

Jeff McMahon: I don't think the average person who buys this record at Wal-Mart is really gonna know the difference or care if it's us or studio guys on the record. They only know whether or not it sounds good to them. And I'm hoping that they'll hear a little something different on this one, and that that will enhance what they already like about Tim's thing.

John Marcus: We're all secretly hoping that this starts a trend with other artists now because it'll become a cool thing to use your road band on your record.

Robert Allen: Tim's clearly upset some people in Nashville with this album already, but I think you'll find that it will pay off for him in the long run. I love the fact that the more Tim bucks the system, the more the fans and radio love it.

John Ward: Will this record sell a trillion copies? I hope so, but that's up to the audience. I think it's probably the best record Tim's ever done, but maybe that's just because we all feel like we have an emotional stake in it. Tim has always been that guy that kicks the door down and drags people with him, so who knows? Maybe this will be the record that changes the way the Nashville sound sounds. It's definitely coming from the heart, and if that comes through to the audience, it ought to fly off the shelves. The band went above and beyond the call of duty; they really put their heart and soul into this, and it shows.

David Dunkley: The first time we heard the finished album, it was like, "Wow, we did this." I hear Tim McGraw records on the radio all the time, but I've never heard a Tim McGraw record on the radio with me on it. I've never been to a store where the Tim McGraw record's playing with me on it. I mean, I'm forty years old and I've never heard myself on the radio. I've dreamed about this since I was a little kid.

Dean Brown: Denny and I were riding bikes through the parking lot at one of our shows and people were tailgating and every single car had a different Tim McGraw song playing. I said to Denny, "Won't it be funny next year when we're riding through and

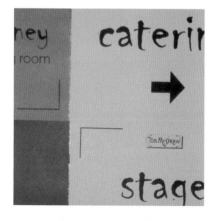

people are playing the songs and it's actually us playing on them?"

Byron Gallimore: My hat's off to Tim for taking a chance on doing something that very few people in his position would have the guts to do. But that's just the way Tim is. When he decides to do something, he just assumes that he can pull it off whatever, and in this case he did.

Scott Siman: One of the fun parts about Tim is just watching where he goes. When Tim started out, he was kind of an outlaw and a rebel and an outsider, and then I think he came to understand the music industry and understand his part in it. Tim isn't striving to be different for the sake of being different; he's striving to be different for the sake of being better. It's not just to say, "Hey, look how self-indulgent I can be. "I think Tim's at that spot in his career where a lot of country acts have had to strive to continue to be relevant and to continue

you get, the harder it becomes. And I think Tim's keenly aware of that.

When you've been doing this for a while, it's easy to get cynical and take things for granted. But I'm feeling really excited about this record, and a lot of that's because of the energy that I'm picking up from the guys in the band. I've known and loved these guys for such a long time, and I know their character and their honesty and their integrity and their dedication and their loyalty. So to be able to go in and finally cut a record with them—and for it to come out so amazing—has been a great experience that has been good for everything in our lives.

You've got to keep challenging yourself if you want to stay alive as an artist. I still don't think I'm anywhere close to being as good as I want to be, but with this record I feel like I've taken a big step toward the kind of music that I want to make. I think it opens the door for being more creative, and it allows us the freedom to try all kinds of new things. Now we can be playing one night and somebody can come up with a cool lick or a cool sound, and we can say,

When you do this kind of thing, you're always juggling a certain amount of confidence and a certain amount of doubt at any given time. No matter how successful you are, all of those doubts are always going to be somewhere in the back of your mind.

before, and I think that's going to take the whole thing to a new level.

This whole project has gone way beyond my original expectations. Making this record topped any musical experience that I've ever had and opened the door to doing all kinds of new stuff and lots of different kinds of records. It feels like we've stepped up and opened a door to a whole new place. It's a new level of inspiration, a new level of confidence. To me, it feels like I've really dug my feet in now in my career, and now I'm just going out there and making music.

When you do this kind of thing, you're always juggling a certain amount of confidence and a certain amount of doubt at any given time. No matter how successful you are, all of those doubts are always going to be some-where in the back of your mind. But I'm way past letting that stuff keep me from doing what I need to do. I've still got goals, but most everything I've ever wanted to do, I've done. There are all kinds of things that I would still like to accomplish, but if I had to quit tomorrow, I'd be happy to settle for having great kids and a great family.

I look at myself as the lucki-est guy in the world. I'd still be doing this even if I was playing in bars, so to be able to be up there rockin' in front of 20,000 people a night is way past anything I could ever have imagined. If none of this had ever happened, I'd still be playing music some-where. If I had a house gig in some bar in Louisiana, I'd still be doing it, you know?

faves

JOEY SUPAK Since 1998
Drum Tech

FAVORITE TIM SONG: "Things Change"
FAVORITE SONG ON THE NEW ALBUM: "Red Ragtop"
FAVORITE SONG EVER: Little River Band's "Reminiscing"
BORN: Austin, TX August 19th

JOHN WARD Since April 1994
Front-of-House Sound Engineer

FAVORITE TIM SONG: "One of These Days"
FAVORITE SONG ON THE NEW ALBUM: "Real Good Man"
FAVORITE SONG EVER: Frank Zappa's "Village of the Sun"
BORN: Charleston, WV September 25th

JOHN PRESTIA Since 1999
Guitar Tech

FAVORITE TIM SONG: "You Get Used to Somebody"
FAVORITE SONG ON THE NEW ALBUM: "I Want the Best"
FAVORITE SONG EVER: John Lennon's "Imagine"
BORN: Bay Shore, NY July 4th

JULIAN KING Since 1992
Engineer

FAVORITE TIM SONG: "Don't Take the Girl"
FAVORITE SONG ON THE NEW ALBUM: "Red Rag Top"
FAVORITE SONG EVER: The Hollies's "Long Cool Woman (In a Black Dress)"
BORN: Charlottesville, VA November 16th

BYRON GALLIMORE Since 1992
Producer

FAVORITE TIM SONG: "She's My Kind of Rain"
FAVORITE SONG ON THE NEW ALBUM: "She's My Kind of Rain"
FAVORITE SONG EVER: (Can't decide, there are too many great songs)
BORN: Paris, TN March 23rd

TIM McGRAW Since 1967
Artist/Producer

FAVORITE TIM SONG: "It's Your Love"
FAVORITE SONG ON THE NEW ALBUM: "She's My Kind of Rain"
FAVORITE SONG EVER: Hank Williams's "I'm So Lonesome I Could Cry"
BORN: Start, LA May 1st

PHOTO CREDITS

CHAPTER 1 THE VISION
Title page and all photos: Marina Chavez, Miami, FL 2001 and Lincoln, NE 2002

CHAPTER 2 THE DANCEHALL DOCTORS
(1–12) Marina Chavez, Lincoln, NE 2002; (13) Montage photos by Marina Chavez, Albuquerque, NM 2001; Glen Rose, Rayville, LA and Tampa, FL 1998; (14) John Maginnis from 1996 Spontaneous Combustion tourbook

CHAPTER 3 THE JOURNEY
(1) Marina Chavez, Lincoln, NE 2002 (2) Album Covers 1992–2000 (3) Marina Chavez, Miami, FL 2002 (4) Contact sheets courtesy McGraw art archive (5) Glen Rose, rehearsals at MTSU, Murfreesboro, TN 1998 (6) Tim rehearsing in a church basement 1993, photo by Jeff McMahon (7) "Angry All the Time" during Soul2Soul Tour 2000, photo by Marina Chavez (8) Unused photo from *Everywhere* shoot; photo by Russ Harrington 1995, Pine Bluff, Arkansas; photo by John Maginnis (9) Band photo, tour rehearsals 1995, Pine Bluff, Arkansas; photo by John Maginnis (10) McGraw archive, performance 1993 (11) Tim, Darran, Denny, John onstage Tour X, 1994, photo by Kelly Wright (12) Tim, Fan Fair 1996, photo from fan (13) Tim, Fan Fair 1996, photo from fan (14) Tim, Tim McGraw On Tour 2001, city unknown, photo by Kelly Wright (15) Tim, Tim McGraw On Tour, closing night, Nashville, TN, photo by Kelly Wright (16) *A Place in the Sun* press photo; photo by Russ Harrington 1998 (17) Billy, Denny, Tim, Jeff on band bus, New Orleans, LA 1999 before Bread and Water show at Tipitina's. Photo by Glen Rose (18) Tim, 1994, photo by Jeff McMahon (19) Polaroids from *Everywhere* and *A Place in the Sun* photo shoots, photos by Russ Harrington (20) Billy Hawley, Tim onstage at George Strait Country Music Festival, Detroit MI 1998 (21) Live shots from 1996 tourbook. Photos by John Maginnis (22) *A Place in the Sun* media image, Bethlehem Steel Plant, Bethlehem, PA. Photo by Russ Harrington 1998

CHAPTER 4 THE MUSIC
(Cover photo) Marina Chavez Lincoln, NE 2002 (1) Song Chart John Ward 2002 Allaire Studios (2) Darran, Marina Chavez Lincoln, NE 2002 (3) Bob Minner, Marina Chavez Lincoln, NE 2002 (4) Byron Gallimore, by Dean Brown 2002 Allaire Studio (5) Denny Hemingson, Marina Chavez Lincoln, NE 2002 (6) Billy Mason, Marina Chavez Lincoln, NE 2002 (7) Darran Smith, Marina Chavez Lincoln, NE 2002 (8–10) Erik Lutkins, Ricky Cobble, and Julian King, by Dean Brown 2002 Allaire Studio (11) David Dunkley, Marina Chavez, Lincoln, NE 2002 (12) Billy Mason, Marina Chavez Lincoln, NE 2002.

CHAPTER 5 THE PLACE
(Cover photo) John Ward, Allaire Studio 2002 (1) Dean Brown, Allaire Studio 2002 (2) Map with signatures courtesy of Joey Supak (3) Dean Brown, Allaire Studio 2002 (4) Dean Brown, Allaire Studio 2002 (5) Dean Brown, Allaire Studio 2002 (6) Denny's Steel Guitar, Dean Brown, Allaire Studio 2002 (7–11) Studio Instruments, John Ward and Dean Brown, Allaire Studio 2002 (12) Candle, John Ward, Allaire Studio 2002 (13) Lamp, Mark Hurt, Allaire Studio 2002 (14) The Bar, Denny Hemingson, Allaire Studio 2002 (15) Candles, Dean Brown, Allaire Studio 2002 (16) Sherman Halsey, John Ward, Allaire Studio 2002 (17) Menu Card and Denny's Welcome Letter Courtesy of Denny Hemingson (18–22) All pictures courtesy of Jeff McMahon, Denny Hemingson, Dean Brown, and Joey Supak, Allaire Studio 2002 (23) Joey Supak's Journal, Allaire Studio 2002 (24) Dean Brown's journal, Allaire Studio 2002 (25) The Bar, Jeff McMahon, Allaire Studio 2002 (26) Dean Brown, Allaire Studio 2002. Ambiance at Allaire Studio provided by Landy Gardner and Chadd James. Thanks, guys.

CHAPTER 6 THE RECORD
(Cover photo) Jeff McMahon Allaire Studio 2002 (1-2) All Photos courtesy Jeff McMahon, Allaire Studio 2002 (3) Darran Smith, Jeff McMahon, Allaire Studio 2002 (4) Byron Gallimore, John Ward, Allaire Studio 2002 (5) Rick Cobble and Julian King, John Ward Allaire Studio 2002 (6) Drums, John Ward, Allaire Studio 2002 (7) Tim, Jeff, and Byron, Dean Brown, Allaire Studio 2002 (8) Billy Mason, Anonymous, Allaire Studio 2002 (9–13) All photos courtesy of Jeff McMahon, Dean Brown, and John Ward, Allaire Studio 2002 (14–16) Photos courtesy Mark Hurt and John Prestia (17–20) All photos courtesy of John Ward and Jeff McMahon, Allaire Studio 2002 (21–22) Photos courtesy of John Ward, Allaire Studio 2002 (23–30) All photos courtesy of David Dunkley, Jeff McMahon, Denny Hemingson, and Dean Brown, Allaire Studio 2002 (31–32) All photos courtesy of Dean Brown and John Prestia, Allaire Studio 2002 (33–38) All photos courtesy of John Ward and Denny Hemingson, Allaire Studio 2002 (39) Dean Brown, Allaire Studio 2002 (40–46) All photos courtesy of Jeff McMahon, John Ward, Dean Brown, and Joey Supak, Allaire Studio 2002 (47) Dean Brown, Allaire Studio 2002

CHAPTER 7 THE DELIVERY
Title page and all photos: Marina Chavez, Miami, FL 2001 and Lincoln, NE 2002

CHAPTER 8 THE FUTURE
(Cover photo) Marina Chavez, Miami, FL 2001 (1) Marina Chavez, Lincoln, NE 2002 (2) Marina Chavez, Miami, FL 2001 (3–10) Clockwise from top left: set list; Tim walking to the stage 2001; Tim dunking, Billy watching Ames, IA 2002; Montage photos by Kelly Wright various tourstops 2001, 2002; Tim in front of video wall; Darran, Billy, John backstage, Scranton, PA; wall backstage; Dean, Zep Lyster backstage 2002. All taken by Kelly Wright (11) Tim, Scott Siman, backstage Nashville, TN 2001, photo by Kelly Wright (12) John Ward, Jerome Thompson, Manny Mederios, Billy backstage Detroit, MI 1998, photo by Glen Rose (13) Tim entering stage Marina Chavez 2000 (14) Tim's dressing room photo by Marina Chavez 2000 (15) Marina Chavez, Miami, FL 2001 (16) Empty seats and *the* hat box that has survived unbeatable odds, by Marina Chavez 2000

All photos are the exclusive property of Tim McGraw. Copyright © 1989, 1990, 1991, 1992, 1993, 1994, 1995, 1996, 1997, 1998, 1999, 2000, 2001 and 2002. No photograph may be reproduced in whole or in part without the express written permission of Tim McGraw. All rights reserved.